LONGINGS

poems

LONGINGS

poems

MUKULIKA BATABYAL

New Delhi | Calcutta

HAWAKAL PUBLISHERS PRIVATE LIMITED
70 B/9 Amritpuri, East of Kailash, New Delhi 65
33/1/2 K B Sarani, Mall Road, Calcutta 80

Email info@hawakal.com
Website www.hawakal.com

Cover designed by Bitan Chakraborty

First edition (paperback) July 2022

ISBN: 978-93-91431-17-4 (paperback)

Price: INR 150 | USD 11.99

For my darling boy, Tigi, *whose love is what I carry with me everywhere.*

FOREWORD

Longings is Mukulika Batabyal's first poetry collection. Though she has only begun showcasing her work, and her writing is raw and requires whetting, I believe the strength of her writing is its raw and rugged texture.I am grateful to *Hawakal* for launching *The Young Poets*, for representing fresh and unique voices, which is a happy and thoughtful gesture, and for selecting Batabyal's debut collection for this series.

Longings depicts the primal desire to belong and become. The poems in this collection are written with a kind of vulnerability most evident in us as we seek romantic love and human companionships. As most of these poems are composed during the Pandemic times, they exemplify eros and desire for attachment, essential elements that mould human relationships in a post-Pandemic world. In a recent conversation, Mukulika tells me that she ardently believes, "home is a time, or people, but hardly ever a place. And the only aspiration has been to fill this void and to find that home. I have pursued love, all forms of it – familial, platonic, sexual, and romantic and I have found home but never one to return to. And in my head the yearning has grown, and my heart longs only more painfully." Thus, in the absence of a permanent home, Mukulika takes solace in words – sometimes fragmented, sometimes in images, sometimes in sentences that gradually form prosodic meter.

I'm certain Batabyal's writing will reach out to millennials struck by the pangs of online dating, all the while fighting patriarchal gaze. Her poems are also reflective of years of trauma, longing for maternal love, and touch of the familial. Mukulika's ability to turn household objects of regular use as material for poetry is unique, and I see it as an essential feminist tool in writing one's experiences. Questions of home, motherhood, belonging, and becoming remain crucial to this collection. The figure of the Mother, even in her absence, has inspired generations of feminist writing. In Mukulika's quest of learning about her mother, who she lost when she was a child, is a search for herself – a journey to fetch herself out of wilderness. I wish Mukulika the very best for her journey ahead. I am hopeful, this collection is a first of many to come.

SHAMAYITA SEN
June 2022
New Delhi

ACKNOWLEDGEMENTS

To write poems because you love it, and suddenly one day you are writing an acknowledgement page for your chapbook. Life happens and how! Sometimes, you have good days, and then they are followed by better days that bring you so much joy. On the weekend I had my first poetry reading, that very Sunday, Hawakal came up with this life-changing opportunity, and my dear friend, a senior poet, and mentor, Shamayita Sen, very kindly suggested that she would like to recommend my name. A few days of compiling, and hours of editing gave birth to this small collection that I hope will be the first of many.

I could have never imagined this if not for the kindness of a few people. I would first like to thank the publishers at Hawakal, Kiriti Sengupta and Bitan Chakraborty, for coming up with this brilliant idea and turning it into an opportunity. I could not think of a better place to submit my first manuscript that makes me so vulnerable. My heartfelt gratitude to Shamayita Sen who thought my poetry had some value, and pushed me for it. Without her motivation and guidance this could not have been possible. I would like to thank my parents who never understood this knack for writing but always encouraged me to keep at it, and my friends who have read my drafts even in the wee hours of the morning.

And as far as being grateful goes, I would have to thank all the places that have been so kind to publish my poems in their anthologies. My first poem, which was published by Calcutta Apologue in 2019, was only the first in the list of opportunities I did not believe would come my way. Soon after, I received a Commendable Mention at the Wingword Poetry Prize organized by Delhi Poetry Slam. A few of my poems have been published in the *Gideon Poetry Review*, *The Pangolin Review*, and in an international anthology curated by *Gideon Poetry Review*. Last, but not the least, I would like to take a moment to appreciate my soft, hopeless romantic heart that still has and always had so much love to give that it found a way to spill on to paper. Thank you.

CONTENTS

WHAT IS THIS LOVE?

To love someone
so wholly
and to not be able to give it
is a tragic waste.

You would think
sending out your love
into the universe
would have some ricocheting effect.
Like a bullet, it would come and shoot you
right in the heart.
But love isn't solid;
it's liquid,
it spills
from the container
that holds it
rolling down your arms, your torso
down your legs
on to the earth
and slides into the mud;
the universe soaks it up,
it is waste after all.
All this love
turned fossil,
and mud.

Or, maybe they turn into wildflowers,
that no one cared to foster
which bloom yellow and red and orange.

Wasted love turned into wasted flowers.
Yes,
that's how the universe warrants poetic justice,
and back to waste it all goes.

LOVE AND WAR

Love
that is fostered
lingers longer
and festers faster
with stickier scabs
that tears and tugs
at the skin.

The stale sweatsweet smell
from your pores
that haunts my olfactory glands
clogs the memory hole
choking at my throat.

My stomach churns
with chunks of feelings swallowed whole
blocking my intestines
with air bubbles that run around in circles
looking for the exit door.

You left a war brewing inside of me,
are you coming back for more?

THE CLOCK GOES ROUND

This afternoon I had a dream.

I was a child
and my room was full of light.
The underneath of my bed was clear
and my mother was humming a song:
it's a pretty day,
we never have to leave.
There were so many books stacked by my bed,
she picked up one to read to me.
And then she looked up at the clock,
it had to go one full round.

And then,

I was a girl,
and the light had begun to feel too hot in my room.
The underneath of my bed
had but one skeleton
with a blue hair band on her head.
In the radio there was a song:
Oh a sunny morn!
What a day for a beach party.
The books on my bedside were gathering dust.

I picked up my mascara
and glanced at the clock,
it had goneonly a quarter.

And then,

I was a lady.
The room was filtered sepia
and the underneath of my bed
had gathered a few skeletons –
there was my unresolved issues with my mother,
my lover with his wristband,
and the lover before that.
The girl with the blue hair band was almost gone,
turned to dust.
Alexa was playing me a song:
Afternoon has turned to pass,
nothing seems to ever last.
The books by my bed had outgrown the table,
and the clock had gone half a round.

And then,

My hair was a nice mix of grey.
The insides of my room glittered in the fading sun,
the underneath of my bed had additional skeletons–
one wearing my father's wrist watch,
one wearing a wedding band
the other half of which appeared planted on my finger.
The sensory device was playing a song in sync with my mood:
In all the hours of the day
have you noticed,
the evening takes the longest to stride
through its ever changing crimson array.
Then the device rang shrill,
it was all but a quarter left.

And then,

I was a child again,
fragile and without teeth.
But my body seemed to heavily ache.
It was a noir
for there was no light
seeping through my window pane.
I could no longer look under my bed,
but I think there was only dust.
The screen across my bedside
kept playing a constant tune:
A beep, a beep, a longer beep.
I think someone's phone rang:
You have at long last come home
in the midst of night,
I have stood waiting
an eternity.
The stories in the books by my bed
had all lived as a part of me.
The doctor walked in
and said it was done,
the clock had gone its full round.
He recorded the time— 00:01

PLAYING HOUSE

I have seen mothers
like grandmothers before them
just as their mothers
being initiated into the game of house.

The game of house is a simple game
in which every girl child ever born is an unwilling participant.

She is conditioned into the procedure as a child
with her fancy oven-shaped culinary toys,
and her make belief partner who goes to the market
while she stays back home and prepares the meal.

She is taught to dream
of a life and a career
but never to leave the thought
of a loving husband and beautiful children far behind
lest she forgets the game designed for her to play.

The game of house is a simple game
where even women in a postmodern world
after the numerous waves of feminism
are forced to put their trust on patriarchy to know better.

Where women—
strong, weak, brave, resilient,
vulnerable, fastidious—
all of them reach their fiercest potential only in motherhood.

Where
juggling between a home and a career
is the only balance to be attained
lest time runs out.
or she menopauses
and is left old, alone, and unsafe.
Lest she has no house to play.

The game of house is a simple game
where a woman is at the center only till she has made the house
and then she is uprooted,
silenced,
pushed out,
into the periphery
outside the circle
leaving the game as it is
only for another to come and play.

RECIPE ON HOW TO PERFECTLY COOK A FEMALE TO SATISFY THE MALE GAZE

Ingredients:

Extra virgin olive oil, meaty breasts, curd. Corn flour, biscuit crumps, eggs, powdered onion and garlic for batter. Salt and pepper to taste.

Method:

Heat a pan on low flame.
Take a cup of extra virgin olive oil.
While the oil is heating
take a plump fatty piece
preferably the breasts (of course the breasts!)
beat it hard to flatten it out,
to give it a controllable shape.
Marinate it with curd.

Set it aside and get to the batter.
Take some corn flour and biscuit crumps
mix it with salt, pepper,
powdered garlic and onion.
Beat an egg,

will help in fluffing up the batter.
Dip the meat in the solution
but, aah!
Who has time for so much foreplay?
Jump into it already!

Take the marinated meat
Submerge it in the heated extra virgin olive oil
and dip your hands into the heated pan
since you lack patience
and devour it.
Hot, oozy, soft, battered meat.
Perfect meal of a female served.

SUMMER, 2021

It is the summer of 2021.
Sultry afternoons are about staring at the ceiling fan,
and some occasional hopeless thinking.

I reminisce summers gone—
packing bags to return home.
Those were happier times.
When air was cheaper,
and affection was as heavy as the weight of your
body when you jumped up for hugs
without sanitizing first.
Can you imagine!

They obviously no longer feel real anymore.
Life has now become a perpetual summer vacation
except we must replace the word vacation with the
word nightmare.
The urban dictionary with its repository for
millennial vocabulary
should add pandemic to the synonyms of nightmare.
They now mean the same.

Google tells me, my part-time lover is currently
1009.6 kms away.

But what separates us is no longer geography;
that would have been simple.
A few days before he came down with the virus
he complained to me about chapped lips
and all I could imagine at that point was his plump
soft lips against mine.
His lips must feel drier now
probably more chapped.
But in my head and heart they still feel as alive as the
time I could touch them.
In these moments my mouth usually break into a
faint smile
but I have to immediately close my eyes and remind
myself to be grateful,
in all this, he is healing, that's all.

My thoughts are sometimes interrupted by
ambulance sirens
or maybe I have started to imagine them.
Everywhere I look, I see loss
and I wrap my arms around myself a little tighter.
The amount of suffering shrouding humanity adds
on to my guilt
and my physical fitness feels like a burden
What if I could give my health to my lover?
Would I volunteer?
And all the times I have joked about death,
do I want that?
Have I really ever wanted that?

TO RESEMBLE MY MOTHER

At 16
my grandmother mentioned to me
how I resembled my mother
in my limited appetite for human interactions.
She told me a story
where my mother had locked herself in her room and
read out loud
just to be left alone.

At 23
my paternal uncle
who hadn't seen me since I was a child
was amazed at how much I resembled her physically.
He told me I looked like a version of her who hadn't
aged a day since they first arranged her match for her.

At almost 26
over the sobs of my broken heart
my cousin tells me
I resemble my mother in my intensity to love.
she tells me how she had left brown letters too,
a diary with recipients unknown.
Her favourite books reeked of unfulfilled love,
a lifelong yearning that painfully broke her.

When I am 40,
if I am 40
and I have outlived her
will I resemble her then?
Will I resemble her still?

DATING APPS

On dating apps,
my body starts conversations.

Likes rake up
on the picture
that has a little show of cleavage.

The algorithm
sets my net worth
which is almost negligible
because I will always be that woman
they met on an app
and what could be expected of me
besides looking pretty
and having a fastest-fingers-first compliance to sex.

My wit is a lore
and my desires limited to my sexual fantasies.
My opinions are a cacophony to be jarred
lest they block out the moans.

Almost every "hi"
sets a timer
to the next "what are you wearing?"

But my lonely heart
thumping beneath that skin
always softens the blow
and negotiates another chance with me:
"What if, this is the one?"

LOVERS

In my art
and my heart,

through all the crumbled pages that I have flipped;
in the cracked tunes of the transistor
and the charred bread from the toaster
and the spilled juice
on my grandmother's embroidered table cloth;
the whoring universe within me is begging—
chaotic, explosive—
pushing, shoving, embracing, accommodating
all the lovers in my life I could not keep.

NOVEMBER

It's November
and in a day the golden sun
has aged a season.

Were the kids here last night
for their spooky story session
or did that happen a year ago
when we went pumpkin carving
to a small pretentious party
with scary faced lanterns and humans?

The stench of the damp floorboards
numbs the freshness of the golden light
seeping in through the cracks of the closed window,
begging: open.
Did it rain last night
or last monsoon
when you detangled your giant fingers
intwined in mine
just like the raindrops that escape every time I try to hold them?

The light does not hurt my shoulders,
it glistens instead,
and the crust of my dried skin

feels like it could crumble with touch
like the dried leaves that crowd the window sill.
The almost crescent bend in my neck
where your face rested perfectly
like the two halves of the single moon
going around the earth to form a whole
is now but a half-hollow crater
that could ashen in the beaming sunshine.

It's November
and in a year
I haven't aged a day
since you left.
Your musky perfume still consumes the air
and the damp from last monsoon
has map-shaped coffee stains
from your caffeine addiction
but was it you that left my hand
or did I unlock the door
to rid myself of the loneliness
that had started to resemble you?

NEED

Sitting on a suspension bridge
in the thick of the night
freezing,
breathing smoke,
it chanced upon me how stability is all we need.
Like the rails of the bridge to hold on to
and for someone to look at us and genuinely mean it.
It doesn't matter if they don't make us feel like the water
lashing in a storm
against a boulder in the ghost moonlight
or, like all the four elements of the universe colliding together.

A twinkle
flickering warmth
soothing breeze
Some firm land
calming water
is all there is to need.
The rest is just excess, really.

"THE RUNAWAY DINOSAUR"

In a starry night I lie on my bed
with a foam pillow beneath my head,
I look up at the ceiling and stare,
so many things in the world I dare
and then I hear the lullaby you used to sing to me.
it was about two birds flying free.

Wishing with all my heart I close my eyes
hoping you would appear in disguise
and tell me that story again
about how two little boys beat up the bully, Ben.
You would tell me I was brave enough
to take on the world that called me daft
and when my lips bled you would be
sitting by my bed singing a sweet symphony.

My every scar you would heal
and every monster you would kill
only the little devil under my bed you would keep
to give me company when you finally leave.
Every winter you would tuck me tight
and in a blizzard you would never let me out sight.

Every inch I grew, you would measure
and constantly assure me I was a treasure.

Nothing made me worthy of you
but you still believed I deserved to top the queue.
My eyes, my smile, my heart was perfect for you;
and the reason behind it? I had no clue.

When I open my eyes I still see
the starry ceiling staring at me.
The lullaby however, continues to play
and with its melody I drift away.
Oh mother, your love is what pushes me along
can I not keep you a little while long?

Title taken from *The Flash* (Season 02, Episode 21).

TWO CUPS IN A SINK

Do stars align on the nights
lovers have insurmountable distance between them
trying to network a path for both their hearts to meet
for a rendezvous

or, do lovers have to zigzag between the twinkling lights
to escape the cosmic plan that cannot bear the weight
of very full hearts?

Or, do they just sit across from each other on a bed
warming their feet under the same blanket—
toes occasionally brushing,
the thick air scented of musky vanilla that settles around them
from the heat of happy hormones—
while sipping tea from cups whose vapors disappear into
the pores of hope

or, do they meet only in the sink
with tea stains and leftovers
when they leave the cups there?

HEARTBREAKS AND WORMHOLES

When your heart breaks,
wormholes open
and through them you begin to free fall.

Down you go
aiming for a rock bottom
only to know there is none.

Exhausting hours later
when your body turns unresponsive
a stimulus shoots to your brain
signalling a compromise.

But you imagine
heartaches cannot physically compromise,
only to see a glimpse of its literal physical
manifestation—
a sore zit on your cheek.
Then there are two
and then, five.
The trapped pain from the wormholes begin to ooze
out through the portals
where you were once kissed.
They have festered
infested with bacteria and dead skin cells.

Then you think of the moon on a full-moon night
when you can see the black on its surface
that protrudelike acne scars.
And you begin to wonder,
Are zit scars and craters on your face,
tales of conquests too?

INTIMACY

Very late
on Friday nights
I start craving intimacy.

I scroll through my contacts
make some very desperate calls
to men who have chosen,
very consciously,
to either friendzone me
or slut-zone me,
or both,
or none.

Most of the calls ring to no answer
or they are declined.
It fills my being with regret
hating, beating, half-begging, promising
to never make that call again.

But again
it's a Friday night
and I start craving intimacy.

OF WINTER

Of last rays of the fall sun.
Of eloping souls on the run.
Of bare feet and weighing hearts.
Of crimson love being torn apart.

Of glimmering radiance on thy face.
Of making peace with distaste.
Of falling leaves and fading hues.
Of the oncoming solitary season blues.

Of dusty mantel being dusted clean.
Of winter arriving on a submarine.
Of the depth of whiteness in the garden.
Of the frosted feet of the distressed maiden.

Of beauty in all dead things to sing.
Of a happy song that they don't call spring.
Of the verity of harsh cold-winter breeze.
Of brazen tales naked of crease.

Of the celebration and joys that give some reason.
Of Odes sung to this dead season.
Of the summers and monsoons and all that is bygone
Of happy winter figures forlorn.

First Published in *The Pangolin Review* (Issue 13).

RAMEN IN A STEEL BOWL

I loved Ramen as a kid.
And then I unloved it because it was flat.
Now I love it again.

I usually eat out of a steel bowl, or a steel plate.
Fancy dining sets continue to serve guests.
I usually sit on my bed while I eat.

I indulge with a steel fork which has "Anglo swiss" engraved;
it was a free gift with a watch my father bought ages ago.

I like watching fancy fitness regimes on YouTube.
I try following them.
But I am too middle class for soy milk and almond milk
strawberries and raspberries
whole wheat pasta and whole wheat bread.
I don't really know what brown rice is.
I have white rice for lunch.

I follow no workout routine.
Have no gym subscription
or clothes.
or sneakers.

However, I enjoy walking.
For hours on end.

But it is monsoon now.
So, I eat Ramen and rice
intake carbs
and don't really exercise.
I am unhealthy.

This morning has been rough.
I did not shampoo my hair.
or go for a walk.
I did nothing productive.
My dreams for this morning have died.
Most of this day is done.
What happens to all this time unaccounted for
and all the expired dreams?
Do they die with the time
or do they float in the universe like my Ramen swimming
in a middle-class steel bowl that I eat with a steel fork?

First published in *Poems Around Us* by *Gideon Poetry Review*.

A TOWER, EVERY HOUR

As a 90's kid, I spent most of my Springs
watching birds
collect straws
for their nests.
Springs now are humid, clammy, rainy
and quite devoid of birds
because we need"a tower, every hour."

As a 90's kid, so much of my rural visits were about
ponds,
and ducks and swans in the ponds.
Now, those ponds house concretes,
those ducks, dead to the ground–
probably eaten,
for we need "a tower, every hour."

As a 90's kid, my zoo visits
had at least one mandatory story about some wild predator;
some ferocious lion or tiger,
and their attack on civilians or poachers.
Now, tigers are endangered
with ninety-seven percent of their population wiped out,
but we need "a tower, every hour."

As a 90's kid, I watched Jaws
and was terrified and fascinated
by the sheer size and magnanimity of the shark.
And now:
A "dead shark washes ashore, neck bound with plastic,"
a dead whale had "40kg plastic in its stomach."
C'mon, we do need "a tower, every hour"
As a 90's kid, I went to the University in the late 2010s
and I had written a piece on a little bird in my first year there.
Sadly,
the little bird doesn't nest there any longer,
neither do so many other birds.
Migratory birds have stopped visiting,
God knows if they are still living or have gone extinct.
Little sparrows no longer frequent
pecking on the glass of my window.
Even then we need "a tower, every hour."

First published in *Riding on the Summer Train* by Wingword Poetry Competition.

AFRAID, MOTHER!

Where are you, mother?
I cannot see.
All I want is for you to come home quickly.
It was so loud that I nearly cried.
She left me saying she had to go home tonight.
Her child was alone and now so is yours,
the world is blazing and there is only chaos.

The sound was so loud mother;
I think it was the next block.
Come home mother, we could run away to the dock.
I am afraid mother, taking refuge under the table.
All I have with me mother, is a pen, paper and bible.
I will be good mother, and say my prayers.
But you have to get home mother,
you cannot be a pawn of theirs.
Come home mother, humanity is bleeding.
The world is red mother; there is no sign of healing.

Published in *Cradle Tales* by Calcutta Apologue.

THE LAST TIME

The last time somebody broke my heart,
it was dawn
and the world did not begin for me the following morning.

My soul was drenched of colours
while the hues of the sun were quickly filling the sky.

I had to walk through the furnace of orange heat
with my bleeding heart in my palms.

And find strength enough to carry
my drained heart almost at dusk
when the crazy colour splash was bidding goodbye.

The last time somebody broke my heart,
my world ended one fine morning
and only began again at night.

Published in *A Book Called Home* by Half Baked Beans, curated by The Anonymous Writer.

MECHANICAL INTIMACIES

Tonight
the primal desire in me
for social interactions
pulsate and convulse;
I feel an urge to mate.
Or, to find a mate.

I want to believe,
I am searching for intimacy.

My calendar
is marked in green.
I am ovulating
my vagina has been throbbing for touch.

I swipe faster
and lose patience quicker;
start conversations
that mostly bare me off clothes
leaving untouched my soul.

I want to believe,
I have found intimacy.

DILLI-KI-SARDI (DELHI WINTERS)

The fabled *Dilli-ki-sardi* gets lonelier once you have *baarish* to go with it. People cocooned around their diffusers and heaters with *adrak wali chai*. Living alone gets you to the bone especially on these days when you brew that cup of tea to sip it alone along with some breakfast that you quickly put together. Your cook hasn't made it so you will scramble a bowl of maggi for lunch, and for dinner, and for all the meals in between. The only place that feels warm is the three layers of blankets you gathered in trying to build a fort against the cold during the thunderstorm last night. But of course, it turned a furnace and you discarded them pretty quickly. Much like the relationships that fall through in modern dating. There is no point in the suffocating warmth of either. It isn't consistent. Best not to deal with it. It always breaks my heart how most women I know go through this excruciating ordeal of putting themselves out there only to be disappointed over and over again.

Everything is tiring. Especially on rainy days. Especially, when no one wants to have that cup of tea with you. When no one is around to share your maggi. To nuzzle your toes under the blanket. Sit with you near the heater. Help you clean all the mud from the balcony. Or, just stay in bed with you. Especially then.

www.ingramcontent.com/pod-product-compliance
Lightning Source LLC
LaVergne TN
LVHW040926150826
845672LV00007B/2216

* 9 7 8 9 3 9 1 4 3 1 1 7 4 *